Giants of the North

A tale in verse by

Jonathon Best

Giants of the North

Copyright © by Jonathon Best
All rights reserved

First Printing: 2018
Revised 2022

Paperback ISBN: 978-0-9953520-3-2

www.jbestbooks.com

Map for the Lost

Giants of the North

'Twas morning and the autumn breeze	- 5
They roared like no man ever knew	- 6
The Oakwood man left no delay	- 7
A mountain moving through the skies!	- 8
Again the giant found its voice	- 9
The mayor, once atop the hill	- 10
The giant plunged in river's bed	- 11
In practise, heavy arrows flew	- 12
With time he slipped into a trance	- 13
The Oakwood man then felt a quake	- 14
His people of the oak wood, sought	- 15
Head down, away from distant north	- 16
The horse had clearly had a fright	- 17
No greater battle, ever penned	- 18
A giant they had labelled 'beast'	- 19
But only one would be so blessed	- 20

Statue and Stone — - 22

About Author — - 24

The Journey Begins...

'Twas morning and the autumn breeze
Did breathe upon the emerald view,
From distant islands 'cross the seas
It made its way to town, then through,
To settle in the yawning wood.

The sun, still in its drowsy mood
Would wake and stretch across the land,
To push away what night had bruised
And dulled with one large smothering hand,
'Till barely more it held its fast.

A flight of birds did overcast
the peaceful town of Oakwood Vale,
Who'd seen no cloud this dark and vast
Lest with it came the storm and hail –
So knew the balance had been thrown.

In shadow of the ones who'd flown,
The farmer's ploughed like nothing seemed
amiss, though, now from valley's throne
The treetops shook while wild eyes gleamed,
And hordes of startled beasts charged through.

They roared like no man ever knew
And still the hooves did trample forth,
In fright of something dark and true
That spread its way from furthest north,
And handed death to all it caught.

Though as of yet, the farmer's naught
could tell of why these creatures fled -
And even greatest theories got
Were nothing more than theories said,
As far from mark they mostly fell.

Now, to the north where monsters dwell
There ventured man of vale's oak wood.
His presence there, he'd no one tell,
As - riding faster than he should -
He clutched a letter to his chest.

The letter told of such unrest
That those of Lakeside had made haste –
For, north they marched their very best
And found the forest laid to waste;
The cause they could not rightly say.

The Oakwood man left no delay
To lend the Lakeside town a hand.
He galloped - though by seventh day
The forest looked a barren land
And neither men nor trail was found.
He searched among the rocks abound,
And then, towards the dying wood.
He found a crater in the ground
Where midst the vines, there lay a hood
With sigil of the Lakeside town.

Our Oakwood man did clamber down
And save the hood attached to cape -
It folded neatly as his own,
Though when he turned to make escape
A tremor froze his beating heart,
And gone were thoughts of his depart.
In fact, all thoughts had left his shore
As from the woods a howl did start -
A deep and rough and angry roar –
Of next events you'd doubt your eyes.

A mountain moving through the skies!
A pinnacle of shrub and rock,
Believe me, for I tell no lies,
And as our man fell into shock,
The giant passed above his head.

To witness you'd have thought him dead,
As till the night, on ground he'd lay,
And when he woke, his heavy head
Ensured that for his haste, he'd pay.
Through blurry eyes he looked around.

Where not much more than dust was found,
The air turned thick as winter stew,
and from the grey, a tendril – round,
did pulse and wriggle as it grew.
A hungry mass of purple vine.

The clearing there left him no sign
Of any which way he should go -
But as the night lost starlight's shine
Behind the harsh onset of snow,
He knew to stay was not a choice.

Again, the giant found its voice,
In chorus bloomed the creeping weed
That helped the snow turn dirt to ice,
And chased our man, who'd taken heed
And fled to distant speck of green.

To Oakwood Vale we change our scene
And witness many loaded carts.
As day to night turned quite obscene -
With weather, missing from the charts -
The villagers prepared to flee.

"To southern land of rocks!" Said he,
The mayor, as he gathered tools.
"Away from shade of cloud and tree
where evil plays us as the fools -
We'll be prepared for when she dawns."

So through the night they steered, by horns,
The cattle, which now dragged their home
Across the plains of foreign morns,
'Till mountains shared the orange dome
That rose once more against its will.

The mayor, once atop the hill
Did indicate a passage, thin.
Ahead they would march one day, still,
And all could feel upon their skin
The morning warmth turn piercing white.

A quake did blur their very sight
And many thought a dream they saw,
For with a howling flood of fright
The villagers could think no more -
A giant! clambering 'cross the field.

The men, did many objects wield
And staggered forwards, bones a clack.
The woman with their curdled shrills
Stayed far behind, and shimmied back.
The creature growled and kept its course.
It flung great vines without remorse -
The purple veins absorbing life.
The men, now soldiers to endorse
A safety over child and wife
Did scream and charge, full steam ahead.

The giant plunged in river's bed
And sent a wave fast headed south.
Within were vines that, far from dead
Did search for eyes, and tongues in mouth,
To drain them dry of God's own gift.

A second group of men did drift
And falter to a sudden halt.
Through purple vines their eyes would sift,
In search for those who did revolt
Against the forces of the dark.

But through the growth they found no spark
Of people who they once did know.
In place of bodies, vines now park,
And so the men turned, reared to go –
And fled till night, without a rest.

Hunters, archers, best of best,
And all of those who held a hilt,
Did lie in wait atop a crest –
No time for shelters to be built –
For giants soon would siege the throne.

In practise, axes shattered stone
and heavy arrows whistled by.
A pouring rain sent chills to bone
as thunder gathered in the sky.
Towards the cliffs the giants walked.

Jump back to where our story forked,
And let's check on our Oakwood man -
With bottled courage now uncorked -
He searched to find the Lakeside Clan
And fight the common enemy.

Though, anywhere, he'd rather be,
Than lost and horseless in the snow.
He held his sodden cape tightly
But had no clues on where to go,
So kept his pace and blindly ran.

He hoped to find a caravan
Of Lakeside folk, fast in retreat,
Where he could help them forge a plan
Whilst grabbing something warm to eat,
But at this speed he'd not a chance!

With time he slipped into a trance
And knew for not how long he'd fled,
But saw he'd made quite an advance
 As once again, the flowers bled
Their colour, 'bove the purple sea.

Then something unexpectedly
Appeared in close, just to one side.
A great stone creature, tall was he -
And wide as twenty cows were wide,
Though motionless and quite confined.

Around its legs wrapped purple bind
And followed course up past the hips.
The vine constricted eyes, now blind -
 Held fast great arms and stony lips
of giant, who'd been caught mid run.

And just ahead, another tonne
Of rock, was fastened to the ground.
Its pose did show he'd wished to turn
And aid the one our man first found.
Now giants both, a feast did make.

The Oakwood man soon felt a quake,
As from the trees just exited,
Came giants! Tentacles would break
As more vines than a shoal of squid
Did viciously snatch at their feet.

Now, in an awe-inspiring feat
Our man did leap and arms out throw.
He gripped at all his grip could meet -
The moss, grown thick on giant's toe,
And took his place among the herd.

A thought, that once had seemed absurd
Approached our man, who'd understand –
The monstrous roars that he had heard
Were nothing more than cries, as land
and lives were stolen by the weed.

He wished the giants to be freed
From vampiric and spreading plant.
Although these creatures couldn't bleed
They shared his hurt, that much he'd grant -
With quickened heart, there struck a thought.

His people of the oak wood, sought
a way to slay these beasts of stone –
So, of the truth they must be taught,
Before a massacre of bone
and rock be undertook in vain.
He wondered how to make a rein,
As, knowing not of how to spur
these beats, he feared their haste would wane,
So thinking fast, he gripped the fur
And towards the mantelshelf he'd start.

What he did next would earn no heart -
Our man took flint from pocket's depth,
And lit the moss where cheeks did part -
The giant, bellowing his breath,
Did shriek aloud with quickened pace.

You'd think the giant in a race,
It scampered on with such a speed!
The Oakwood man held tight his place,
And watched the ground twixt them and weed
increase, as they migrated forth.

Head down, away from distant north,
Towards where cloud and storm still brew,
Beneath where towered mountains dwarf
the Oakwood men and women, few,
Who stand their ground, prepared for war.

Defence did swiftly prove a bore
As day and night did blend to one -
Though none would dare speak of the chore,
As so far, there'd been onslaughts none -
And no one wished to break the spell.

Another day, then night befell,
The people growing weary still -
And those with fuel left in their well
Did lay more traps beyond the hill.
The tension they could hardly bear.

Without a change, the clouds unfair
Brought thunder, shaking air and ground.
Between the rocks, there clopped a mare -
One recognized as lost and found.
An empty saddle knotted tight.

The horse had clearly had a fright,
Yet through its thinning, ashen face
The stable master knew it, right,
That Oakwood man had gone at pace
Far north, aloft this very mare.

Where auburn coat showed spots of fair
and patchy skin, the purple weed
had taken root, and, blooming there
did 'cross this strong and handsome steed -
The stable master bowed his head.

Not far behind the horse's tread
Were silhouettes of shrub and stone,
To secret valley, they'd been led -
While rain and thunder set the tone
A battle broke 'tween stone and man.

All knowledge of their hurried plan
was lost, as spears and arrows flew.
Distinctly they'd protect their clan
And never let these monsters through.
Great loss to both sides would descend.

No greater battle, ever penned
Could you in myriad books there find.
This fight did seem to never end,
And those who lived would lose their mind
in torment, of its very sight.

There settled now the darkest night,
Where rain would briskly turn to snow,
And lightning gave the only light,
Except for where new flames did grow
As torches browned and burned the moss.

The Oakwood people suffered loss
as bodies fell from mountains high,
Or ended up a bloodied gloss
Sprayed up towards a giant's thigh
when caught beneath the stone stampede.

At valley's floor a child did plead -
His sinless tears turned snow to rain,
and in the dark he saw a weed
that sensed the bloodshed 'cross the plain,
And stretched and thrived on such a feast.

A giant they had labelled 'beast'
Did push into the stony pass,
And snapped the weed, then movement ceased
amidst the fire-ravaged grass
and growths, between its rock and bone.

Like thunder, chorused howls did drone
and shake the mountains, far and wide.
The giant fell - his own tombstone -
And blocked the valley with his hide -
The purple weed could find no hold.

A battle cry from young and old!
The creatures here could yet be killed.
All thoughts of giving up were sold
And all but pleading child were thrilled,
For he had seen a kindness there.
He kept his eyes locked in a stare
With stone and fire, midst the snow.
For giants he now said a prayer
And wished, for all, the weed would go
And leave the warring sides to rest.

But only one would be so blessed -
Or cursed – to witness such a scene,
Our Oakwood man, despite his best,
Approached, as all that he'd foreseen
did crumble in a pyre of flame.
Collapsing under guilt and blame,
He wallowed as more giants fell -
He heard his brothers yell and maim
and kill, as they depicted hell -
And stronger did the weed become.

With dawn there came the final strum -
The last man standing, bleeding out.
A giant sat with arms gone numb,
Unable now to fight or shout -
Together, they would fade and die.

The Oakwood man could nought but cry,
Regretting so, his slow return.
And now in mud and snow and lye,
The vines he'd fought so hard to spurn
Came twisting towards his beating heart.

Statue and Stone

The graveyard of ten thousand stones-
A maze to match the sky-
Was riddled with the blackened bones
Of centuries gone by.
The stones did reach to realms of dreams
As vines then grew in cracking seams,
But never, knew they why.

The purpose of these stones so proud
Was something left unread,
Yet somehow, through the smoke and cloud
A statue, surely dead,
Did rise the tallest of the flock,
With buried feet among the rock;
Showing stars his head.

And there, the winged creatures glide
Atop the noxious veil,
In envy of the beautified,
empowered statue, pale.
The other stones not blessed as he-
Much shorter than this statue be-
Were shunned by sun and gale.

To beast that drags is belly raw
Whilst scavenging the heath,
And breathes what filters through its jaw
And eats with rounded teeth.
Oh, to be as the statue, grand-
To rule atop this wretched land;
Alas, it crawls beneath.

Yet as the evening passes by
The statue – leaning thin,
Does sigh a most unnatural sigh
Of loneliness within.
No company from mud or stone;
Above the earth he stands alone,
No friend nor next of kin.

ABOUT AUTHOR

Jonathon Best was born in the coastal city of Portsmouth, England. Inspired by the surrounding castles, forests and caravan holidays, there's no doubt that his childhood there has contributed a great deal to his fantasy based imagination. Now living in a tin shed in Perth, Western Australia, the contrasting landscapes and lifestyle offer new perspectives and flavours that he can't help but mix into his writing.

As well as writing, Jonathon enjoys exploring new lands, hiking, and having vivid dreams.

To read more poetry, visit Jon at jbestbooks.com

Author's note: For readers of the 'Amazon paperback edition' of this book, an e-book copy can be downloaded for free with the same account.

If you enjoyed this poem, please consider rating or reviewing it online.

Contains over 40 poems

Now available at

amazon.com/author/jonbest

jbestbooks.com

www.ingramcontent.com/pod-product-compliance
Lightning Source LLC
Chambersburg PA
CBHW020432010526
44118CB00010B/544